WHAT BOOKS PRESS

AN IMPRINT OF

THE GLASS TABLE

COLLECTIVE

LOS ANGELES

ALSO BY PAUL LIEBER

Chemical Tendencies (Tebot Bach 2011)

INTERRUPTED BY THE SEA

PAUL LIEBER

LOS ANGELES

Copyright © 2018 by Paul Lieber. All rights reserved. Published in the United States by What Books Press, the imprint of the Glass Table Collective, Los Angeles.

Publisher's Cataloging-In-Publication Data

Names: Lieber, Paul.
Title: Interrupted by the sea / Paul Lieber.
Description: Los Angeles : What Books Press, [2018]
Identifiers: ISBN 9781532341403
Subjects: LCSH: Theater--Poetry. | Families--Poetry. | Pizza--Poetry. | Dead--Poetry. | American poetry. | LCGFT: Poetry.
Classification: LCC PS3612.I333 I48 2018 | DDC 811/.6--dc23

Cover art: Gronk, *untitled*, watercolor and ink, 2018
Book design by Ash Good, www.ashgood.design

What Books Press
363 South Topanga Canyon Boulevard
Topanga, CA 90290

WHATBOOKSPRESS.COM

for Gwenn and Sam

CONTENTS

Another Ocean Poem   3
Navy   5
Pismo Beach   6
My Father's Cousins, The Ones I Never Met   8
Breaking and Entering   11
#7 Ocean, Film Noir   13
Lips   15
Gray With a Tint of Subway Blue   17
Turbulence   19
Enough   20
Homesick   22

The Fallacy of Comparisons   27
Problem On Stage   29
S and M   31
Sum   33

Dear Robert Dear	35
Mob	37
Humphrey, Always in Response	39
Another Earth	41
Cirque du Soleil	43
????	45
Free Association	47
No Borders On Dementia Lane	51
Chosen	53
Mom's Monologue	54
My Mother Whispers, "Why Are They Clapping?"	56
The Place Where New Life Never Begins	57
Bridge	59
Mother is a Stopped Clock	62
I Just Spoke to Philip	63
So the Call Arrives from Hospice	65
Los Angeles	71
Encounter at the Market	73
Patrick's Roadhouse	75
San Juan Capistrano Mission	78
Carpets	80

I Mark Time With a Pelt-Covered Drum	87
Spell	90
Memorization	93
Matters of Matter	95
Morning	97
Minecraft	98
I'll Bury It in the Catacombs	100
Lost Cause	107
Algae	109
Boundaries	110
The Original Drink	111
Company	113
This is Not Jalama Beach	114
Acknowledgments	117

INTERRUPTED BY THE SEA

*"On the coast you have
one main neighbor."*

—WILLIAM STAFFORD

ANOTHER OCEAN POEM

I called you "God,"
not even a manifestation.
I called you "God,"
a blurt, a slip,
an innocent mistake
and you,
a solution,
a wet link,
a churning sway,
a swan, a flirtatious
swing on shore,
a flare of white,
a slide of your wing,
an approach, a retreat,
a beckoning.
I called you "God"
as if you weren't elusive,
as if you were the writer,
not the first page
or the cover, the binding.
I called you "God"
because I can't grasp
indifference, enormity,
frivolity and on and on,

as primitive as the beat
of every heart,
as complex.

NAVY

It rained last night. It's as clear as
1950 when I had pink skin and hadn't yet
daydreamed murders. The hard lines
of Catalina can be traced, and the cliffs
behind me so defined each fold begs to be
named and you reflect a triangle of light,
your blue so dark, my mother would have
called you navy when she could see. You're
post-storm, twitching with mini-waves
scratching the shore. You had a difficult
night of water bruises. I'm so tired of
pricking myself. You ask why I keep
returning, breathing waves.

PISMO BEACH

I'm with your long-legged
blood relative surging down
as far as far is
with a crystal rinse
spilling from fog,
a stretch of sea
I'll never see up close.
My dog sniffs, circles, digs,
a jerky predator of smells.
To the right
the lanky porno-pier
sticks it into your belly.
Your shore dotted
with shells and rocks,
an equitable dispersal,
a socialist shore
and you, the generous
lush-gowned-event,
mist and faint
mountain lines
then apparitions,
memories, dreams
in ethereal strands
undulate to sand.

Some deal was made
at the start: Keep them
rolling at all costs,
never mind pettiness, murders,
white collar crimes or illegal wars,
just keep those waves
coming and they do

MY FATHER'S COUSINS, THE ONES I NEVER MET

Yes, you can personify the vast blue.
Here they come again, barreling

over one another, twins, cousins—almost
identical, hardly identical—they spread across,

keep spreading, a series of curls, then rupture . . .
Just as I become familiar with the bulge of blue,

it collapses. And ten strangers appear.
The seagulls pick the sand . . . A black-banded

one approaches, nonchalantly waits
as I reach into my pocket to hand her

a quarter. She backs off as if insulted,
but it's all the change I have.

Fluff white smooth stuff, she
struts as if she'll live forever; stops,

looks closer, asks, "What makes me me,
and you you?" I tell her to read Spinoza.

An overweight seagull swivels his head
towards me, then the water. He squcals

like my son, strolls on twig legs, gains
momentum, then he's in the clouds.

A family of four waves hurries to their
destruction. A family of three tips in, crumbles,

and the ocean, with its balconies,
rolls its tiers in a dreary narrative,

a repetitive tragedy. Another lush,
uninhibited file ends in a liquid flare . . .

Now sleep, yoga, a blue golf course
with no players. It's the rhythm

of your breathing, so they say.
It's really death slapping the shore.

And what about my heart that sped
at 165 beats for a loveless hour?

They attached a monitor to measure
the surf in my veins. The doctor

said, "It's not life-threatening."
He didn't know we were already dead,

breaking his news like a wave
spilling over itself.

BREAKING AND ENTERING

At your mouth this morning,
you're smooth, calm, a soft growl.
Do you know my mother is 94?
Eyes failing and would barely
hear you tiptoe today. Your slight
surf, stronger than Long Island Sound,
but careful not to wake up sleepers,
surreptitious breaking and entering,
pawing at the sand, a collection
of whispers sensitive
to the ears of mussels and clams.
I think a friend hates me or does he?
How can he not? Who loves, hates;
who hates, loves; the old emotional ocean
with your blue singe, your sway,
taller now, your unabashed
moods. When a roommate had a few
days left to cough and smoke cigarettes
between gasps on an oxygen tank,
she pleaded to be taken to the desert.
You're my desert, my mountain range,
my café in the east-west village,
a cobbled street in Paris,
the casbah in Tangier,

my tumbler of sea,
a mosaic of titillation,
my stretch of impossible.

#7 OCEAN, FILM NOIR

Blacks, whites, grays,
a rinse of modest waves.

A morning of rest before
or after the murders?

You leave clues. Footprints.
I'll interrogate this lump

of seaweed later, before you
swallow another witness.

Are you mourning the gulf spill?
Don't plead innocent.

Your life-giving solution
gave rise to killers.

A saline accomplice.
The black of you.

Another clue: sand blankets
the walkway and bike path.

Why the cover-up?
You're not saying a word.

Just singing your runaway song
of breakage, rush and indifference.

I won't bring up the drownings.
I won't bring up Stephen.

Your lure, your seduction,
draws me back mornings.

The truth is I get lost
on land. Your gridless map

is simple. No hills, turns
or freeways. We'll tar you.

LIPS

Yes it greets as it rises in almost unison,
the wet long salute as if we'd forget
this triumph on the planet. Tourists
in winter clothes travel light years
to the wet borders, stride as surfers
paddle in the tinted-lightest-blue-
gray-green. More surfers march toward
the breaking sounds for their perfunctory
entry with the ocean bending, now waist
deep, shoulder, one jumps and paddles,
misses the wave as I scribble on
Elizabeth Taylor, a photo appearing
in an ad for her perfume. I jot on her eye,
across her nose, approach the moist lips
that break across her face. Yes, they rise
like surf, two swells where America
disappeared, where Montgomery Clift
deserted his homosexuality for a few hours
to kill Shelly Winters in "A Place in the Sun."
The height of these breakers could murder
any depression, assuage your anxiety, pull you
away from torment into the swirl. One surfer
takes us with him, covers us with salt water,

so cool, we're chilled, all our needs
forgotten, our sexual appetites dispersed.

GRAY WITH A TINT OF SUBWAY BLUE

Out swing dolphins heading
north, rocking, and you
like a blue breeze, a drenched blanket

they take for granted.
The sky painted extra white
to match your splash of lips

bursting along your chins.
I've returned from NYC.
The subway would arouse you.

Fresh water with salt, flounder
with trout packed next to blue tuna.
Gold fish rubbed bellies with cod.
We were starfish, showcased on the F train

as my son looked out the subway window
at the steel mingling with coral reefs.
Graffiti scrawled everywhere.

Coney Island, your distant cousin,
was a dish of urban drool.
City dwellers drowned

their congestion. They swam
in their debris and were ecstatic.
Squamous cell carcinoma metastasizing
as I speak.

A motorboat whizzes by in the distance.
The dolphins disappear in your depths.
They grab the D train to Malibu.

Do you really exist or
are you a vast illusion?

You try to imitate yourself
but can't. Today you're in your high tide
costume, calm, closer than ever.

I see right through you.

TURBULENCE

I owe you an apology—
as if I could make a collage
reflect your gallop, feast,
honesty. No, no collages
here, you're complete,
wrapped in the horizon
and a sandy shore,
between the rushes,
the little tragedies
and their resolutions
that disappear into
brine, and underneath
that blue plunge, the webs,
the interminable endings,
ungainly wet fractions—
our first step toward infinity.
My neck swivels
to take your surfaces in
so they can reside in me
for the day. I beg
for peace and completion
like every greedy soul.

ENOUGH

Oil tankers, lit,
one shaped like a fish hook

another, a tiny umbrella
glow on the horizon

ecstatic as if they discover
our coastline. Further out,

the long grimace
of a Channel Island

gasps for air
as Sam gathers pock-marked rocks,

avoids anemones that booby trap
the shore. Touch them and they don't

explode but get smaller, smaller,
like shy children. We are anemones

with legs as we hike through
this platter of sand while

the swirl of blue black clouds
and clouds, inescapable,

blanket, quilt and gather
our compliments—

then move on.

HOMESICK

I'm facing north,
the ocean over my left shoulder.
That would be the Pacific.
On the east coast, the Atlantic
would be swaying over
my right shoulder.
Two blocks away my wife and child
argue and another 2448 miles east
stands Parker Jewish Memorial
Nursing Home where my mother
free associates.
I skim the ocean, its swells,
channels and salutations.
The surfers look for thrills.
I'm just looking. They wait
for the wave in hiding.
Everything below the surface
rises and bursts open,
a billion epiphanies.
Where will they break?
Surfers misjudge the future
like the rest of us
as cells collect and spin in their
assignments: water cells

adhere to water while humans
stick to humans until
these smooth collisions.
Foam spreads,
temporary maps dissolve.
I sit cross-legged
and my calves tingle, asleep
until I change positons,
maybe move back east
and wake the entire body.

*"When I go away from you
the world beats dead."*

—AMY LOWELL

THE FALLACY OF COMPARISONS

I walk with a slice in each hand,
one from Ray's, the other Joe's,
down mugger-free 6th avenue
and I could be comparing
Vernal Falls in Yosemite to
Misty Falls in Sequoia, I could
be comparing my high school girl
to my college one, an arm around each, a kiss,
an embrace, an entry with proof
not possible, nothing proved, except
frivolity. There might be parallels
to the fall of Rome on this,
my last day of atheism. The start
of belief in a thin or thick crust with a splash
of red sauce, speckled with parmesan
and a nibble, the slightest nibble
of corn meal, yes a tingle of corn meal
humming in the dough. But wait,
not in either slice, that's in
Two Boots Pizza on Avenue A.
For now it's tangy or not, one
with traditional tomato sauce
in one bite while marinara with
garlic is poised in another and

this contest rages with no
winner in sight, but I'm rounding
6th Avenue, heading for Bleeker Street Pizza
where they combine crust not too thin
but on the thin side with a spicy
but not too spicy…. or then again I can
break away from orthodoxy
into a mozzarella rapture
with dervish basil spinning on top,
erupting in an operatic climax.
I swing onto the street in my oven
of anticipation as heavenly bursts
of ricotta, oregano and
the thinnest slices of pepperoni
begin to shower, to pour down
into the belly of Waverly Place.

PROBLEM ON STAGE

She says, "move forward
not side to side, stand straight
I'll come to you," and I ask
how about when I kiss your neck
and she answers, "just bend,
as long as you're lower."
The next day I receive a note
from the stage manager
to keep my mouth closed
when I kiss her although I thought
it was, but I might have
moved from side to side.
The word from another producer
is she's really upset and that
this producer is being pressured
by the other producer
for me to keep my mouth closed,
but this actress has always been difficult
and when she pulls away
from the osculation scene
out of loyalty to my wife although
in the scene before, my wife
says it's okay for us to make love,
when she brakes and breaks away,

I lean on the counter and wait
for her next line which is marinating
in her stomach area, spiraling
up her esophagus as it churns
and churns and by the time
sounds form words and they
are released through her open lips
they've lost all logic,
all semblance of meaning,
but in fairness they are personal enough
and I'm thinking Lee Strasberg lives,
although he too was misunderstood.
And the knowledge that her actual
sister is homeless and an addict
no longer rouses my sympathy
when she withdraws from
the closed lips of my character,
the lips her character
is supposed to find irresistible.

S AND M

He says in every relationship,
one plays the sadist, the other,

the masochist and the sadist
in me knows what he is talking

about while the masochist in me
perfunctorily agrees, as we both listen,

seated, patient for him to finish,
aware that he has a low threshold

for contrary views. My masochist
wallows in his sentences while

the sadist fantasizes pushing him
into traffic. We think, two sides

of a coin, while the sadist
picks at a cuticle on the thumb

of my right hand until a trickle
of blood waves a white flag.

Then the masochist sucks
the thumb, cleaning up the mess

like a serf or an obedient spouse.
By this time he ends the lecture

and we applaud. Some of us
stand, those who really want

to be on his good side.

SUM

There's her pale clear skin
covering the skull of another
who even wears her hair length,
the crouch, the bend in her spine
at the same angle.
It's odd to see the bone
in the bridge of her nose
displayed by this boy.
Such concentration in focus
in the corner of the café, by
the dark haired, falcon-like girl
with her visage glued to the screen,
considering and reconsidering.
It's her focus, yes. I'll never find
her impression of anything,
the one that changed
the thing she described into
the thing she described,
like Brando in the car scene
with Steiger, how Steiger's
choice diminished him
while Brando's made him
larger. Listen for her accent,
Russian mixed with German

and English in a delicate rasp.
Listen to her legs. Find them
on this teenager skipping
in front of you. Where are
her eyes?

DEAR ROBERT DEAR

So Robert calls after
his interview on TV,
where he never laments
the death of his wife,

the one he was accused of killing
and spent a year in the hole waiting
for trial. So he wants to know
how he came across

and of course I'm on the spot
because I love the murderer
in him and me and all
the motorcycle rage within us,

but don't agree with actual murder
and he came across, well, as
an amalgam of Jackson Pollack,
Charles Manson and Norman Mailer

and who was she anyway?
Certainly more than the "morose looking
flab eyes who was on her tenth
scam marriage." So I tell him

he was refreshingly authentic,
always charms with rawness,
talent and leather vulnerability
as unrepressed souls can,

a wounded instigator
neglected to the core,
left with a brand of honesty.
And yes, you came across

as a possible killer or a likely
victim but always a cherished
love object, and, yes, we can
love the murderer.

He considers my response,
covering so many tender bases,
and decides we ought to work
on that David Rabe scene we talked about,

the one we're too old for but
emotionally right, where two guys
stab their arms with needles
to prove their love for the same girl.

MOB

He was a well-spoken
drug dealer, living with
a girl whose father
was connected and
friends of his father
were on their way,
on their way
to the couple's apartment
on the top floor of our tenement,
on their way so the couple
fled and left the door open
for breezes,
for looters,
for neighbors,
for my girl friend,
an abstract expressionist
who suddenly swelled with materialism.
She raced up the stairs
to snatch a chair
before a neighbor
could grab it,
an ornate peacock seat for
princesses. I helped her
haul it,

intoxicated with
the easy theft,
our minds dissolved.
We were insects.
We were electric
currents,
flowing from a Persian rug
to a toaster, to a vase.
My downstairs neighbor,
a grammar school teacher,
stacked Italian plates.
The swiftly spreading virus
sang a chorus of,
"the couple will never return anyway."
I found two Dylan records
between thoughts,
tucked under one arm, under the other,
Count Basie or was it Miles Davis?
The music blared as we all
returned to the apartment for
more and more until it
lay there stripped
with no curtains left
to block the sunlight.

HUMPHREY, ALWAYS IN RESPONSE

Bogart settles on the couch.
I settle beside him,
waiting to see
how he reacts to the legs
across our living room
with its matching plaid lampshades
and curtains.
There could be an avalanche
set off by her calf,
the heat spilling in,
the empty coffee cup.
We pool our thoughts,
challenged by the moment.
Anyone could knock.
The telephone might ring.
Suddenly we're suspects.
A memory ignites, never invented
never to show off, not even to show
during the inquiry by the detective
in this generic, bare, 40's police station.
Neither of us is pleased.
In the restaurant we run into
friends we have known forever:
you can tell this by how well

Bogey lies,
how truth
resides there.

ANOTHER EARTH

A duplicate earth
hangs in the sky, visible
with the exact history
and in the same moment your double
lives an identical life,
a mobile mirror who
reassures you you're not alone.
A spaceship will be headed for
empathy and for a price
I can embrace my self-loathing, self-loving self
who didn't accomplish, did accomplish,
who slept with identical women.
The one beaten up on the corner
of Montgomery and 176th street,
a fight we were expected to win.
Intimate images will rehash
carbon copy impressions,
omniscient gods for each other,
we'll reminisce about the dead,
share memories of the cherished ones,
a breathing thesaurus for one another's phrases,
phases, every thought before every erection,
even those of kissing a guy
though we had no desire

but the image would sneak into
the puzzle of our teenage minds.
No, no secrets between us,
only the ones we both
were never able to face.

CIRQUE DU SOLEIL

We're here to be astounded,
to marvel that we're capable
of more than bacon and eggs
with toast to dip in coffee,
more than naps or clocking in
from 9-5. We can flip in space
more akin to rubber bands
than Manhattan schist.
These bodies, as flexible as
forgiveness, as godly swerves
that fly on trapezes and
mount each other, palm to
palm, and up the boneless stack
they stretch and leap, twist
faster than you can count
the rotations, and their devotion
to pliancy never doubted.
I confess, it's wasted on me
like fireworks, ice hockey and opera.
Forgive me, but give me
a ride on the F train with
the undisciplined, the underpaid,
the sleepy. Let me slouch
with the unrehearsed

as we rush down
that hole in the ground
in unmatched colors
with sweet stumbles,
uncoordinated bumps—
the un-choreographed at risk
as we race toward
a closing door.

????

A guy in front of me
jumps in a taxi and I
yell hey that's my cab, but it
isn't. It's his but I'm
convinced it's mine.
So I yell again until I realize
I'm not next
as if awakened from a dream
and he says,
as he enters the cab,
"it's okay," reassures me
the way I reassure
my mother who thinks
she's in her apartment,
the one she left five years ago.
Have you ever revealed more than
you should, mistaken a friend as intimate?
Have you ever walked through a glass door?
Has your son ever gouged your eye?
Has your mother called 911 when you knocked
at the door? She can't
recognize your voice.
My cousin witnessed his mother, father
and sister shot, killed.

He pretended to be dead.
He still pretends.
Do you think this is melodramatic?
Do you think this isn't the truth?
I did.
Then I didn't.

FREE ASSOCIATION

He interrupts my monologue
to interpret the Savannah sparrow
perched on the window sill,
speaking to him more deeply
than my problems, the sparrow
landing on the outskirts
of therapy, but having flown within,
steers our attention
to those transient miracles
that flit from branch to window sill,
those colorful excursions into
the soul, while I lie, still steeped
in my hundred-year-old epic,
grandfather's flight from his wife
to another, sealing grandmother
in a loony bin, dad in a Manhattan
orphanage and on and on. Listen to
the squawks, squeaks and chirps.
There's really no choice.
They need to get out.

*"We're all dreamers;
 we don't know who we are."*

—LOUISE GLÜCK

NO BORDERS ON DEMENTIA LANE

She calls from the nursing home
to tell me she's at the cemetery,
visiting her father, and wants

to go to the Grand Concourse
and it's easy to yearn
for the apartment that overlooked

Yankee Stadium, overlooked
that green deception,
the possibility of extra innings,

but she's stuck in this morbid cemetery
or hospital prison so we meander
through beds and tombstones.

Yesterday she taught arts and crafts in Paraguay,
wanted my dad to come by
and sure I'd like a few words with him,

chat about the Great Depression,
the parallels to today. We can discuss
insanity, the context, how today it's cool to say,

I love you. He'll preach that communism
in the 30's was the choice of a thinking man.
I'll agree and break the news

that electric shock is back in fashion.
Mom visits Elizabeth now,
an old friend in Florida and wants me to hail a cab.

We could all ride to Rego Park,
order those fresh sesame bagels,
but now she's angry for locking her

in this God-forsaken-place and
how did I get the office number
anyway? I tell her I know

all her thoughts
and fancy dance steps. I tell her
I know all her numbers.

CHOSEN

They made her watch the books
in the library on Broadway, but

the cows in the library, she thought
were harmless, began licking her face

and were about to eat her so she's
frightened and pleads for me

to stay so I am at her side
with her mouth open as she

breathes, her jawbone sharp,
and she, so alarmingly thin

as she dreams of the man who
calls and says, "of everyone,

your voice is the softest, no screams.
I've waited for you so long

and finally you answer."

MOM'S MONOLOGUE

The G3 button gets you a small hot chocolate,
one for her and one for me then
through the automatic opening door
into the blinding light
and I listen to how we can't blame
men on busses and the subway
after work when
young girls lean on them
and they get erections.
She is so understanding and sympathetic
to their arousals as she continues,
*then fights break out. The men
can't help how it happens* and I
am all ears. *What did I do
to my daughter? I had a bad breakdown.
They visited me. I broke down
and they would visit me.
I think I see some of your white hair
and I can see the panel walls.
Make sure you don't get locked in here
by mistake! If I met your wife
in the street I wouldn't know who she is.
Someone said I had a bad breakdown.
They were afraid I wouldn't make it.*

I won't have an eye operation.
They destroyed one eye,
those bastards. Hum any melody
and I can play it on the
piano. Don't tell the social worker
I'm depressed. They will medicate me.
Those medicines will turn me
into a man. Listen to them.
Hear how their voices are lower.
Men's voices. It's the drugs,
it transforms them forever.

MY MOTHER WHISPERS, "WHY ARE THEY CLAPPING?"

She longs to speak Yiddish
so I listen as if I understand
why she feels responsible
for her daughter's death. Guttural sounds.
Mom yearns to join the fatalities
of car wrecks, heart attacks
or domestic accidents
but for now hangs out with the living.
It's Wednesday so the crooner entertains.
She's transported,
sways like a fish to the downbeat,
flattened and pale, she finds the melody.
It's a testament to the life of "Fly Me to the Moon."
The crooner has enough for lunch and
blood circulates for another afternoon.
Mom's fingers remember, "Till There Was You,"
as she plays the piano but recoils from
applause as if there is danger,
as if someone might notice the length of her nose—
the morbidity under her skin cream.

THE PLACE WHERE NEW LIFE NEVER BEGINS

Her head lies on the dining
room table, arms crossed,
cropped hair whitens
in the back, neck exposed while

I think of the East River,
cleaner now, only an occasional
shopping cart or tin can swims by.
Two green cushions support her.

I have the urge to kiss that neck,
implore her to continue,
knowing she'll never
hear. She slopes daughterless

in the midst of those dreams,
the ones she can't shake, strangers
taunt her in neighborhoods
she no longer resides in.

She naps with no religion.
No chorus of Hallelujah
after we drop into the river.
We'll float by like the cartons we were.

There's no meaning outside this tank
of furniture and bills.
Her great-grandchild memorizes
baseball facts, knows names

of players from the 19th century.
It's as if batters whack home runs
in the local cemetery. I won't wake her.
This isn't death, just another pause

while a hundred year-old piano
slants on crooked legs.
Our skewed music
waiting to be played.

BRIDGE

She's washed on shore,
thinning like the faded

distance of those bare trees.
She lies, sits, talks, dies

and listens to music
in the community room.

She claps her hands, light
breaking through clouds,

a respite, a mound of glee,
hunched and smalling,

says," the old still party,"
as 800 and 900 year-olds

crowned in New Year's caps
welcome another year.

A woman from the eighth floor
stares with a grin.

Behind her eyes
lies the desert in winter.

Behind her eyes
aren't nursery rhymes.

They're the eyes
of a Chihuahua.

I ask her if she is in the
nursing home or rehab

and she repeats, "rehab."
"Re hab" rolls

in the cavity
of her mouth,

an intrigue about sound,
about surfaces

and her look at me is
a look at my surface:

those titillating colors,
my white hair,

the blood berry red
that blotches my face.

MOTHER IS A STOPPED CLOCK

Have you ever stumbled on one?
The hands at impossible positions
You try to adjust it,
but you wind up
tossing it out
though the numbers are
clear as numbers can be.
Mother's fingers
travel over ivory
as she forgets arthritis and
picks out timeless standards.
But she's lost. She's outlived
her sight… her friends.
She's got me, dependable
as a flutter. She's got me
to answer the broken questions every day.
"Where's my daughter?
Have you spoken to her?"

I JUST SPOKE TO PHILIP

and he was true to reviews,
no frills, polite and compassionate.
He'll pick up the body, burn it,
ship the ashes, and $575
caps the deal and my mother
whose thoughts, so confused
amidst themselves and reality,
but isn't that true for all of us,
but not Philip who offers
his rehearsed, simple style.
His phone picks up messages
24 hours and I, the soon to be
grieving son, or you, the grieving
whomever, don't have to think,
just charge it to MasterCard
and the ashes will arrive 7-10 days later.
I'll take hers past security,
scatter them in Thomkins Square Park
where they'll blow into the lips
of hipsters. The dot.com crowd might
get a taste across the bustling
Lower East Side that no longer exists
except in burnt and buried memories.
Someone once told me all colds are

the result of a loss as I burn
through a dozen tissues.
And what's the remedy? Cry, cry
for one you can barely listen to,
for conversations you never had,
for impossibilities, paranoia,
persecutions and all the anti-Semitism
that found her sharp jaw, brown eye
and blue, cream skin, her frail
and voluptuous body and
for all the hidden mikes
that couldn't trace her whispers.

SO THE CALL ARRIVES FROM HOSPICE

Her husband and daughter
tango in her temporal lobes,

then harmonize
a haunting melody

about absence. My mother's
final days are not kibitzing

in the Borsht Belt,
or playing black jack

at the casino, no,
she toils in sweatshops

during the great depression,
then vacations in camps

where relatives disappeared.
On a lighter side, she recalls

her son with reefer
outlined in his breast pocket

of a stone-washed shirt as she
cries for him to stay home

but he dances away
to the trumpet

of Lee Morgan at Slugs Saloon
the week before Lee's wife

busts in with a shotgun
to murder Lee.

She pleads to stop all desertions,
all bon voyages.

"Let's put the hospice workers
out of work," she seems to say.

Remember the "Bourne Identity"
when Matt Damon wakes up

and doesn't know who he is.
Let's start there.

"Los Angeles is just New York lying down."

—QUENTIN CRISP

LOS ANGELES

A car swerves in front
of the Mercedes in front
of me and the Mercedes
stops and I stop
but the car behind
slams my rear and
I hit the Mercedes
in the rear and we
all pull to the side
of the 101, 3/4 mile to the 110
going south at 6:45 PM
to exchange our dates of
birth and other intimacies.
The guy in the Mercedes tells me
he is attracted to men and
women. I tell him 25 years ago
my wife was crushed in a head-on
and I could only identify
her legs. The woman behind us
speaks Mandarin but cries
in that universal sob and
the registration whispers that
the Ford is not hers. I uncork
a bottle of Milagro
and we drink to our entanglement,

to the 101 freeway,
somber sips for the 40,000
a year killed in collisions.
We pay homage to that deer
mowed down on the 405,
to the possums that blended
with the 90, to the mangled
licensed and unlicensed dogs,
to mutts and pedigrees,
cats, squirrels, coyotes
and the seagull that couldn't
take flight fast enough.
The forty proof no longer burns
while the freeway ghosts
dance in the Santa Ana winds, then
relax on our dented hoods and fenders.
We hide the tequila and our mood
when the Highway Patrol arrives
in wool-blended shirts
though the temperature is 98.
We answer questions, thank them
for clearing the battlefield,
hug one another, deflate
our airbags and roll.

ENCOUNTER AT THE MARKET

Ed is less his prostate, unnoticeable
from this point of view while
prostates disappear like tonsils
in the 50s. Dave's is gone, Brian's soon
to be, Chuck's is under surveillance and
mine, age-appropriately enlarged.
We look through our prostate lens at the map
of urinals: Starbucks on Wilshire, Whole Foods
on National, while the empty coffee cup
waits graciously on the dashboard.
There goes Alan off a prostate cliff as Chris
drowns under four trickles of urine.
I inhale deeply, balancing between
the here and hereafter, between a doctor's
pronouncement and saw palmetto capsules.
Ed says if he knew how long sex
would be out, although none of those important
nerve endings were tampered with,
he would have opted for radiation instead,
and I can't help but visualize
him and his wife. Or is it the girl
in the aisle whom he refers to
as his eyes follow her past
pasta and dried fruit,

shrunken apricots and mangoes
withering alongside linguini
before it's boiled, still stiff
and on sale for half price.

PATRICK'S ROADHOUSE

It's a mingling of the dead with
scrambled eggs and hash browns.

A way to arrange the clutter of a mind.
The civil wars at rest. We're at

the edge of a continent. Back in heaven.
The counter I sip at has been leaned

on for decades and the wooden booths
alongside windows alongside

the Pacific could make me weep
for booths, counters, for when the train

stopped here, for when there was a train.
Oh please, spare us eulogies to diners,

luncheonettes, to collectables. Here's
a framed copy of an old sailboat

with the white crust of a wave, and
no wind to move it, no, no winds in here.

Tulips next to a chess set, next to sugar.
Photos of what was and never was.

There's the Palisades in mud a thousand
years ago. A "Royal Air Force" sign and one

for "Bigger Hill." Renaissance style copies
of sketches with renaissance garb among

pseudo-antiques. These gargoyles, oils, and
a wall lit with easily forgotten sayings

create a forest from pawn shops where I
wouldn't buy a thing, but I lose myself in

this labyrinth the way I can lose myself
in a broken woman. I climb four brick stairs

to the stained glass chandeliers where
checkered floors bounce off a poster,

"Cat on a Hot Tin Roof, "by the late Tennessee
Williams, starring a dead Paul Newman, at odds

with a dead Elizabeth Taylor. Listen to the surf
creep to the counter. A street lamp is a stud

with a French flag wrapped around it,
like a scarf, like my dead uncle Jack,

adorned with an ascot, ready
to light up the room.

SAN JUAN CAPISTRANO MISSION

The chipped façade of cream brick.
The uneven plaster reminds me
of my apartment on 17th,
those little hills for floors,
the toilet in the hall and
dreams of the tenement swaying.

Forget stiff interpretations
of the bible and the slaughter
of infidels, stay with the mortar,
stones and age, the adobe couches,
those motherly laps
in the garden
away from the burn
of sun and the mission
of this mission.

I hear my father through the archways:
"Religion killed half the human race."

I stroll into the gilded chapel
as narrow as that flat downtown
but the ceiling, with its primitive
beams and mismatched lines, climbs

to the heavens and Latin chants
swirl so,
so I pull up a tier
and pray
as involuntarily as any seduction.

The winding chant pulls me further
to those holy stories, to the creepy almighty,
calling, and I, obedient music, am summoned

past the rape of aunt Jenny,
past the repairman fiddling with a hinge,
above the bombings to the east.
I'm over the ruins,
above the gift shop,
above the bells.

A single note.
An infidel.
Rising.

CARPETS

A random design of festive people,
both sexes, perhaps paired,
perhaps open, with months

spent under the hidden stars,
the ultimate rebellion against bodies
they happen to inhabit

so they discard
the customary bath, shave or a call
on their nephew's birthday.

They were tossed too many "no's,"
but their conversation,
so easy as they drink

from horizon to horizon.
At the moment, they're strewn
in front of Gold's Gym

where a sinew is a shrine,
where a matching tan workout suit
hugs each burst of a curve.

It's a man's property
so he exercises
his right to harden each tissue.

They rebel against the ordinary
glance in the mirror,
falling hard

for their lines and limbs.
One arches his side to eat
love handles.

Another beeps
his car as I consider
the movie "On the Bowery,"

which follows three "bums."
One, a doctor, is offered
a career in Hollywood

but instead, returns to dream
in a cardboard box.
Do we run out of sky, out of affection?

I dropped off my son
but forgot
to give him lunch money

so I drive back but he's already
jogging with fifty others
in perfect rows, so synchronized,

I think of the Gestapo,
a surrender
to the group, the exhilaration, the expanse,

the smallness as they move together
and I don't interrupt this carpet
of bodies as it sweeps along.

*"People should help their kids
 know decisively which way is north,
 if they know which way north is."*

—WILLIAM STAFFORD

I MARK TIME WITH
A PELT-COVERED DRUM

A python curls behind me, quicker
snakes in tanks, and frogs, with chickens

sleeping outside and in. My son's
science teacher instructs students

from all angles until they
digest a reptile or smell how

the earth doesn't spin out like a thought.
Their bones taste dirt sticking to its axis.

I'm thinking of the years it took me to learn
Wislawa Szymborska's name as I search

for the English teacher's classroom. Follow
the alphabet buildings. The teacher

chats in "L," excited how students
will use English until they die

and, perhaps, after. I'm still not sure
of the difference between the dash

and semicolon. Where do you enroll?
Can I go around again so when Lynn Kahn

invites me to her home, not to mention
the perfect grammar of her invite,

"I won't wear anything when you visit,"
not, "I won't wear nothing—" no, no double

negatives, just the prospect of double
crests and curves that frightened

a simile out of me which called her
and said I was "like sick," but Lynn

is as dead as the Romans. Yes,
the very Romans the history teacher

mentions. Now it's Incas.
Well, she's as dead as the Incas.

I learn my son will be preparing
a meal with the Incas' native ingredients.

Perhaps he'll invite a living girl to share
the red and yellow potatoes,

chili peppers and sweet corn and
to please the gods, perhaps they'll dance.

SPELL

Spelling words check into a hotel
with an OPEN neon sign.
They dream of being sounded out.
It's so early, the before, or
just after the after hours.
My coffee croons,

"naugh ty," "be seech," "an ten nae."
It was naughty to beseech the antennae.
The naughty antennae would
beseech other antennae for a hug,
a hump, any show of antennae affection.

My son will wake gradually,
to a lesson on primitive man,
learn about our ancestors
and if I'm lucky he'll pass
on a fact or two,
how Homo sapiens painted
the first paintings on
a cave wall where

a contour,
an indentation, a scratch
resembling a bird, a tree
or another Homo sapien
and details were added

as the wall took flight
into sky and wings,
perhaps the rapture
of a pattern
like a melody
like the way
he catches my eye with his
backpack jaunt, joining
other doves
in droves,
the repetition
of a few bars
of our wave goodbye
as he runs to beat
the late bell.

Then the class room,
the familiar angle
of the teacher,
everyone tethered to desks,
to the morning, to the
next 3 words, "chief,"
"an xious," and "at tempt."
My anxious father called
every man "chief" in his attempt
to be friendly.

MEMORIZATION

Foreign words hang out today:
faux, bon appetit, cuisine, bona fide,
not schmuck, shlemiel, just ones on
the test, the definitions of sixty,
rendezvous, ricochet, beret
and he doesn't have a reference
if it doesn't relate to the Simpsons.
Remember Miles who sat next to me
in second grade and drew pictures
of ships dipping in the ocean, bobbing
on his desk, alluring, begging
for imitation, seducing me into
those portals, until I penciled
exact replicas of his replicas,
balancing on a wave or two.
Miles breathed life
into mindless copying
while my son mimics sounds
of words but doesn't know
an aficionado and hasn't had a rendezvous
with an amateur next to the bureau
of a bureaucrat who says aloha.
He's too young for a bona fide
bouquet given by any amiable amiga

or a visit to the countries
these words escaped from,
now stranded, to be sounded out
while suffering ennui in a Honda
parked five blocks from the ocean
between Pico and San Vicente.

MATTERS OF MATTER

He studies imperfect triangles,
rectangles, wavy lines
that partition New Guinea, Latvia,
Ukraine, not wars, treaties
and deals that determined
who got which side of what, no,
just land from land,
people from people,
and the teacher
will pass out a blank map
and each country will have a number
and beside the number my son
will write the nation until
the planet is accounted for,
each division with a color
while the Andes and Himalayas
roll on disregarding borders
and the Nile flows though Sudan,
Ethiopia, Burundi, Uganda and Kenya,
never stopping to utter their names
or exchanging an Ethiopian birr
for a Ugandan shilling while
our earth spins with murmurs
of French, German, Spanish,

Italian, Arabic, Yiddish,
and my sister who read them all
floats somewhere,
ashes tossed into the Atlantic
off the coast of Massachusetts
but by now they may be nearing
England or the Congo,
Namibia, Nigeria, Ghana,
or more likely
they rest
in those blessed
unclaimed depths.

MORNING

He rises, runs to the computer:
an early morning infatuation,

a dip in the lake,
a jog in the park.

He runs before sunrise
as if to milk a cow or goat,

collect eggs from the chicken coop.
He runs to the screen

like uncle Jack might run
to a saloon before noon.

MINECRAFT

He's across the hall
building a house with
a basement and stairs
to the upper floor. With
stacks of pale wooden
planks he creates a kitchen,
then tends his garden.
Outside, chickens amble.
Inside, his pet cow circles.
Home is close to the flat
waveless water where
he fishes with flair. Dinner.
He sleeps in the computer
on a stiff-looking bed,
wakes to cut weeds that
sprout overnight. He collects
melons he planted last week.
Occasional zombies strike
when the sun goes down
but he handles them nimbly
with a flick of a finger.
He grows into the screen.
His red hair waves in
the lower left corner.

Roots take hold as he relaxes
by a fireplace, hums
while he considers what might
be in the refrigerator, rises
to prepare a cake. He has
the perfect pixels for flour.

I'LL BURY IT IN THE CATACOMBS

My son plugs into
electronic isolation.

I want to drag him
back a few centuries,

to cross the Tiber River on to
the Pantheon. Pigeons approve

in Trastevere. One starts
towards us and retreats,

a pecking of black and gray
like a 14th century Syrian or Jew

searching for a nibble
on these streets with so many slants,

the ups and downs, the difficulty
of putting one foot in front

of the other,
on this cobbled festival

of church bells.
Shutter windows open

when I grab my son's iPad
and struggle in a tug-of-war.

I could scream *I diapered you,*
wiped that mustard

sauce from your anus.
You're drowning in pixels

and I want you to swim in these streets.
I rip it from him,

run down the block where
a stranger leans on his motor bike.

He understands the rage but not
this thing in my hands

is driving me crazy.
I yanked it from

his abdomen.
See, see his blood drip?

"That the world is, is the mystical."

—WITTGENSTEIN

LOST CAUSE

When you've written a poem
about the pier and you're on
the pier, as I am, it's as if I
walk through the halls of the poem.

Where are the girls
with boom boxes
for whom I predicted doom?
Stoned, homeless, shackled

in marriage?
Where are the sardines
that wiggled for life
on the ledges? Today

mackerel beg for mercy,
twist and shimmy at the end
of their line. Legless, one
leaps into a painting.

I suppose the croakers
and bass swim elsewhere.
The fishermen repeat
in their mostly Latino

numbers. A pelican floats
into a stanza, oblivious
to free verse. The tents
have vanished. My son

had grasped my hand in a rhyme,
asked many soft questions.
Today I'm alone while
tourists trample over

this plank. Where is
the bounce in the grain?
This family speaks Swedish.
They sprinkle their words

over the pier,
over lost quatrains.

ALGAE

Brown bulbs,
charred,
twisted,
resting on sand,
worn swimmers,
carriers of messages.
Each bulb
can be decoded
into a Buddhist chant.
A shrine for sea travel,
for having lived
a soaking life.
Seaweed.
I bow to read you.

BOUNDARIES

the tide is out
leaving a flat plain
an expanse of damp sand
a dispersal of sea weed
those intertwining
intestines stranded
maybe orange
maybe light brown
everything in faded colors
in the overcast seascape
the sun cracks through clouds
running into clouds running into
sea no line between
the up and down the gentle
blanket of waves
caress
rather than rough-house you
two dolphins synchronize their swim north
that rhythmic in and out
and you think they hear
you think

THE ORIGINAL DRINK

I used to think
you were mindless,

indifferent, your white wool
didn't laugh as it broke up

on shore. Those eternal jokes
bundled into surf.

I used to think you were
a withholding uncle

who was before I was
born, when I had no eyes.

I won't ask for more
than your trillion licks.

Kindness swings up and out,
a lullaby of rocks,

a liquid seesaw with the obvious
gifts: seaweed, shells

and the minerals
this body yearns for.

COMPANY

I grasp your wet blue hand,
walk beside you—
my older brother, protective,
vast. You've grown into
the unimaginable, wide, enigmatic.
Do you think one thought
constantly? The thump
of your continuous pounding
upstages my tinnitus,
together a squeaky duet.
Your scalloped throat
rises, says, "it all matters
no more, no less."

THIS IS NOT JALAMA BEACH

The clouds roll, swollen and stained
with eternity scribbled
on their stomachs.
I jog into one, speckled
with a breeze, this hill
covered with stubs,
and the ground,
a splattering of pebbles.
You were molten,
now a chill, the layers
of sandstone that some
might think measure,
but there's nothing
to measure. An abrupt
entry into the beginning
of angles, of smoothness,
of inhales, of edges
and shards. A nameless bird
on stilts, the breakage,
your crisp water voice
and my layer of skin,
all born at the same moment.
It's a primordial cut,
a slice of a planet,

rock tissue, the intestines of bone,
a carving from my brain,
the desert by the sea.
You've captured me with long streams,
with your ocean stuff
and my flimsy narratives.
A train of clouds, of waves.
My tumble of words,
my misfires and your exactness
pair up for a moment.
An audience of rocks.
The applause of surf.

ACKNOWLEDGMENTS

Special thanks for your invaluable inspiration and help: Marjorie Becker, Jeanette Clough, Dina Hardy, Sarah Maclay, Holaday Mason, Jim Natal, Jan Wesley, Brenda Yates, Mariano Zaro

Alimentum: "The Fallacy of Comparisons;" *Angle of Reflection* (Arctos Press): "Problem On Stage," "Sum," "Encounter at the Market," "I Just Spoke to Philip," "Navy," "My Father's Cousins, the Ones I Never Met," "This Is Not Jalama Beach," "Homesick;" *Beyond the Lyric Moment*: "No Borders on Dementia Lane;" *Cacti Fur*: "Mother is a Stopped Clock;" *California Quarterly*: "Another Ocean Poem," "Breaking And Entering;" *Givel Press, LLC*: "Homesick," "I'll Bury It in the Catacombs" (nominated for a Pushcart Prize); *The Moth*: "Patrick's Roadhouse;" *Paterson Literary Review*: "Los Angeles" (winner of "Honorable Mention"—Allen Ginsberg Contest & nominated for a Pushcar Prize); *Poemeleon*: "Mob," "San Juan Capistrano Mission;" *Souvenir Lit Journal*: "Chosen," "Navy;" *Spillway*: "Free Association"

PAUL LIEBER's collection *Chemical Tendencies* was a finalist in the Main Street Rag poetry contest. He also received an honorable mention in the Allen Ginsberg Contest. Nominated for two Pushcart prizes, Paul's poems have appeared in many journals and anthologies. He produces and hosts *Why Poetry* on KPFK radio in L.A. and Santa Barbara. Guests have included Poet Laureates, National Book Award Winners and many known and lesser-known poets. Paul works as an actor and has performed on and off-Broadway and in numerous films and TV shows. He has worked as an adjunct Professor in Creative Writing at Loyola Marymount University and is a facilitator at the poetry workshop at Beyond Baroque in Los Angeles. Visit his website at www.paullieber.com.

LOS ANGELES

POETRY

Molly Bendall & Gail Wronsky, *Bling & Fringe (The L.A. Poems)*

Laurie Blauner, *It Looks Worse Than I Am*

Kevin Cantwell, *One of Those Russian Novels*

Ramón García, *Other Countries*

Karen Kevorkian, *Lizard Dream*

Paul Lieber, *Interrupted by the Sea*

Holaday Mason & Sarah Maclay, *The "She" Series: A Venice Correspondence*

Bill Mohr, *The Headwaters of Nirvana: Reassembled Poems*
BILINGUAL, SPANISH TRANSLATED BY JOSÉ LUIS RICO & ROBIN MYERS

Carolie Parker, *Mirage Industry*

Patty Seyburn, *Perfecta*

Judith Taylor, *Sex Libris*

Lynne Thompson, *Start with a Small Guitar*

Gail Wronsky, *Imperfect Pastorals*

Gail Wronsky, *So Quick Bright Things*
BILINGUAL, SPANISH TRANSLATED BY ALICIA PARTNOY

Visit our website at
WHATBOOKSPRESS.COM

ART

Gronk, A Giant Claw
BILINGUAL, SPANISH

Chuck Rosenthal, Gail Wronsky & Gronk,
Tomorrow You'll Be One of Us: Sci Fi Poems

PROSE

Rebbecca Brown, *They Become Her*
François Camoin, *April, May, and So On*
A.W. DeAnnuntis, *Master Siger's Dream*
A.W. DeAnnuntis, *The Final Death of Rock and Roll and Other Stories*
A.W. DeAnnuntis, *The Mermaid at the Americana Arms Motel*
A.W. DeAnnuntis, *The Mysterious Islands and Other Stories*
Katharine Haake, *The Origin of Stars and Other Stories*
Katharine Haake, *The Time of Quarantine*
Mona Houghton, *Frottage & Even As We Speak: Two Novellas*
Rich Ives, *The Balloon Containing the Water Containing the Narrative Begins Leaking*
Annette Leddy, *Earth Still*
Rod Val Moore, *Brittle Star*
Chuck Rosenthal, *Are We Not There Yet? Travels in Nepal, North India, and Bhutan*
Chuck Rosenthal, *Coyote O'Donohughe's History of Texas*
Chuck Rosenthal, *West of Eden: A Life in 21st Century Los Angeles*
Chuck Rosenthal & Gail Wronsky, *The Shortest Farewells are the Best*
Forrest Roth, *Gary Oldman Is a Building You Must Walk Through*
Jessica Sequeira, *Rhombus and Oval*

What Books Press books may be ordered from:
SPDBOOKS.ORG | ORDERS@SPDBOOKS.ORG | (800) 869 7553 | AMAZON.COM

www.ingramcontent.com/pod-product-compliance
Lightning Source LLC
Chambersburg PA
CBHW060456080526
44584CB00015B/1446